I0622647

Heavy Light

Heavy Light

poems

LaCole Foots

Burlwood Books | Austin

BURLWOOD BOOKS
Austin, Texas
BurlwoodBooks.com

First published in the United States of America
by Burlwood Books 2023

Text copyright © 2023 LaCole Foots
Cover design by Andrea Couch Wofford
Cover photo by Jessica Felicio on Unsplash

Burlwood supports copyright. Copyright promotes diverse voices,
sparks creativity, protects free speech, and creates a society that
celebrates the arts. Thank you for buying an authorized version and
not selling out for a rip-off, and for not trying to make a quick buck
by reproducing or distributing any part of this without permission.
Practicing common decency helps support writers and, well, just all of
us.

ISBN 979-8-9850784-8-0

1. Poetry 2. Relationships—Poetry

All rights reserved. No part of this book may be reproduced, stored
in a retrieval system, or transmitted in any form, or by any means,
electronic, mechanical, photocopying, recording or otherwise, without
prior permission of the author.

to Lisa and Hadassa
thank you for seeing me

Welcome

I may be overstating myself... but that may be just fine.

This collection spans three years and was curated from more than 400 pieces I wrote during that time. The poems tell a deeply personal reflection of navigating grown womanhood.

The year 2020 was filled with a never-ending barrage of emotion and pain and expression and information and... and... My work from that year is entitled **&.**

The next year, we all got our footing and fought through the required personal, professional, social, and physical changes. Yet I found myself struggling to describe it all and maybe fearful of naming the feelings I was encountering. Those pieces birthed the section **Use Your Words.** Finally, with a renewed voice and brightening outlook on the vastness of my experiences, 2022 saw the creation of **The New.**

The poems are in chronological order, with some having only the date as a title. I'd ask readers to check the date and see how the feeling of the poem relates to where you are, what you're living, and when. Perhaps it's all cyclical and maybe we're all experiencing it together. Would you let me know?

As for the title, I thought it reflected the dichotomies that dwell within me—fighting for peace, hating how deeply I love, begging for more than enough, serious levity.

I hope you enjoy the pieces and find something in these pages that speaks to you.

LaCole Foots

Contents

& (2020)   3
She will be (1/2)   4
Friend requests (1/17)   6
Lick (3/10)   7
Awaiting sating (3/14)   8
My love is but a virus (4/1)   9
(6/6)   10

Use Your Words (2021)   13
(1/3)   14
(1/25)   15
Use your words (1/29)   16
(4/6)   17
First thought, first flight (6/1)   18
Who promised you a rainbow? (6/4)   19
One day will be day one (6/10)   20
Seems on brand for me, really (6/10)   21
The vision (11/28)   22
November (12/3)   24

The New (2022)   27
12:45pm on Valentine's Day   28
Observer (3/2)   29
Womanhood (3/2)   30
96 (3/17)   31
92 (3/21)   32
85 (3/28)   33
84 (3/29)   34
Dinner with Lorelei (3/31)   36
74 (4/8)   38
64 (4/18)   39
59 (4/23)   40

First be worse (4/29)   42
37 (5/15)   43
35 (5/17)   44
33 (5/19)   45
The righteous believer (5/20)   46
Pending (5/24)   47
9 (6/12)   48
12 (7/3)   49
Goes the spoils (7/26)   50
A note to self in late September (9/26)   53
Sense (10/12)   54
Single tear on smiley face emoji (11/7)   56
A passing thought (11/20)   57
I don't know who needs to hear this (11/26)   58
Sunday (12/4)   59
...days later (12/15)   60
Unresolved (12/19)   61
Overdue escape (12/28)   62
Estes Park (12/31)   63
Closure (Today)   64

Heavy Light

&
(2020)

She will be (1/2)

It's harder to sleep sober
She hasn't been the same woman
Since last October
She's stronger and weaker
Surprises herself
With her own humanity
And hope sown so deeply
She can't help but to weep
When the world reveals itself
To be even more broken
Than she's imagined

She wants to believe
She wants to love
She wants to bow
Some days
She doesn't know how

It's easier to escape
She hasn't enjoyed the sunshine
Since last May
She's healing and unraveling
Scares herself
With her own depravity
And desires so repressed
She can't help but feel shame
When she finds herself in company
That's even more liberated
Than she'd ever imagined

She has grieved
She has numbed
She has fallen to the floor
Just today
She doesn't want to anymore

She was silent
She was observing
She was learning
Tomorrow
She will be

Friend requests (1/17)

He tried to reenter my life and it felt like a test
This time, I'll pass.

Lick (3/10)

And we don't know how to build this love
We've both been told we should give it up
I've used your name as a placeholder
In mundane recounts of estranged lovers
At dinner parties I feign interest
Though acutely aware I crave the intimates
I was a smart girl who was innocent
And lamented being naive
Now I'm a smart girl who's experienced
And cynicism is all I breed
Bereavement of my innocence
Life was limitless
Still believed in my white picket fence
And now I make my own plan b
Where loneliness is a threat, a death
Where I over invest in my own bed
And leave discomfort for my guests
Can I temper it?
This dependence on independence
How indolent! How benign.
These indifferent heartbeats of mine
How dishonest a soul must be
To seek contentment in defeat

Awaiting sating (3/14)

I want nothing more
Than to want nothing more

My love is but a virus (4/1)

I pray you thrive
And stay alive
And cultivate me still
Where shall I go?
Without a host?
Without a hope to kill.

(6/6)

Am I willing to stop the revolution
Because I'm afraid of losing my position at the master's
feet?

Am I willing to disparage the tactics of the fight
Because I may be positioned for a defeat?

Am I slowing movement towards evolution
Because I don't want to give up my relative ease?

Is the problem me?

Use Your Words
(2021)

No more questions
We certainly have the answers
I've doubted in the past
Equivocated and retracted
I've known the truth the whole time
The conflict within my mind was never mine
Who I thought I'd be and who I was
Who I'd said I'd become and who I am
All different versions of the same woman
All different views of the same plan

You're allowed
To question God
Scream at the sky
Demand to know the truth
And God
Has the right to respond
With pure silence
As do you.

Faith has never meant
The absence of doubt
It is simply a choice
We all make

Use your words (1/29)

Sometimes I'm afraid of my own voice
Because it is fierce and powerful

To placate or satiate a racing mind
It spews words unrefined and dangerous

Sometimes it eats itself
I gnaw on my thoughts
Until I feel I've pruned my ignorance
I'm met with copper flavored ideas
About how the world should be

I swallow it back inside
Afraid of the life that it could make on its own

(4/6)

The hardest part of self reliance
Is knowing the self will change

First thought, first flight (6/1)

The buzzing filament
The only thing that makes me feel again
And I flit towards it
In full
In earnest
I see it
Yearn for it
That light sometimes
Is all that guides
The only pride I derive
The only pleasure driving me
Is in goals I strive to reach

Until I crash
Land on my back
Staring at the sky
Storing up for my next flight

Who promised you a rainbow? (6/4)

So many rainy days
That gray's become my favorite color

The storms often peak at night
Reaching my sleeping eyes
Sneaking light onto my sheets
I see the lightning strike
Rip the sky asunder

I pray. I count
Awaiting the thunder

I used to be afraid
Of the clouds and the rumble
Now I take solace
In watching facades crumble

It made us have a seat
It made it be quiet
And I like it
I do. I like it.

One day will be day one (6/10)

What are you up to?
Oh, nothing much
Just laying on the couch
Wondering
How much of yesterday
I should bring into tomorrow.

Seems on brand for me, really (6/10)

I'd thought of quitting
Just last night
But when I realized
No one is watching the flight

I asked who I'd be cheating
If I didn't try

The vision (11/28)

My only direction for you is to get lost
Finding yourself is a win at any cost
All we have is what's within
The secret sauce
Is that we're just an amalgamation
Of our own created thoughts

Take the long way home
Learn some patience
You ain't procrastinating
The journey is the destination
And who the fuck are we racing?
Who determined the pace
And associated ages?
All these fake expectations
Turn into gilded cages
Where we won't take hold of our own lives
Because we're too afraid
Of what we'd make of it

Trust your hands
Give them time to create
And honor the masterpiece
Even if one day
You decide to throw it all away

Trust your feet
Give them time to lead
Honor where you are
And still be proud
When you decide to leave

Take it from me
I don't have the key
All I have is my passion
And some massive fucking dreams...

November (12/3)

What's crazy is the amount of vices
I let slip back in my life since
I decided I wasn't going to be
That person anymore.

Can there be joy found in sadness?
Gratitude for having the capacity to imagine something
Greater for yourself
Even while you don't have it.

My growth is incongruently rapid
It's low grade madness to revert to old bad habits
I may lunge backwards
Succumb to momentary relapses
Fill the void, Destroy synapses
Clap back, Snap fast
Easily triggered into giving overreactions
Alas, that's the past friend

This is the binge before the fast
The cringe before the laugh
The grin mid gasp—
Tense before relax

And I'm waiting for it
Even horror stories
Have a moment of pure peace
Afore and following the gore

The side that I'm on
Is still to be known
I've seen this scene before
And I've survived like folklore

For forward progress
Here's the process I'm mapping:
Seek forgiveness for actions
Make amends for impacts then
Relax sis.
Streams of consciousness
Aren't always meant to be captured.

Am I allowed to heal?
Who can give permission for that?

The New
(2022)

12:45pm on Valentine's Day

If love is madness
　　Incurable joy
　　　　The vehicle thru which we explore
If love is acceptance
　　Unconditional warmth
　　　　The ways in which we create a home
If love is life-giving
　　Affirmation of humanity
　　　　A lens thru which the world makes sense

Is not the answer
To love as much and as often
As you can?

Observer (3/2)

I want to want you
But I don't think
You want to be wanted by me
Leaving wanting
Woman wondering
Wandering to the brink
Pondering between blinks
What a future of solitude would mean

If the answer is on your lips
Speak.
Return my stolen peace.

If the answer is no, let me know
So I may go, reprieve.

If the answer is yes, lay to rest
The feasting beast of uncertainty

And if you're unsure
If time may be the cure
That too may be your truth
Though no hourglass shows
Things we don't know
It only illuminates routes

Womanhood (3/2)

I have not resolved these questions
Of what it means to be a woman
While both defined and definer
Identity rips me asunder

I am no king
I am no subject
I am no slave
I am no clutch

I am no queen
I am no object
I am no master
I am no crutch

96 (3/17)

I want to fight it, fight something
I need a villain
To pull heroic feats out of me
This state of stasis
Seems to be complacence
What purpose is peace
For someone seeking greatness?
Does that then mean
I'm in a constant race then
To be better, smarter, stronger
Never just being here.

92 (3/21)

When the worry starts to swell
And I feel myself start to be overwhelmed
I have to ask
Do I want to be upset today?
Sometimes I say yes.
And let my thoughts continue
But when I say no
When I choose peace
I feel my body respond in kind
In kindness I'll dwell I suppose
Until tomorrow morning

What woman have you become?
One who basks in her impulses
One who lives in the day as if tomorrow
Will always bring redemption
Tomorrow is a better She
Living between the dual disbelief
"Today is all I have but tomorrow is who I am"
One of her is lying
Meanwhile none of her is trying

Why deny it? Stasis is one of those places
That gives while it takes
The peace eats the war
The pain devours the joy

Who said time is so sacred?
As if too valuable to be wasted
I've watched bodies decay
Life stops for no one.

85 (3/28)

Why do Mondays feel different?
The sun doesn't track the days
The bees only know the season

Being protective of my old clothes
My old form
My old soul
It's all I've known
And she was great, she had to be
Which is more responsible for birthing me?
The change or the person I used to be?
She knew. She knew. And she was right.

I know what it's like
To get a new lease on life
A new chance to be
Whomever I like
And that's scary but I'm brave
I've never run from a fight
Even with myself
Even in the dead of night

84 (3/29)

She prowls and growls
On wet grass and parched gravel alike
New playing fields
Taking leads in buildings and on hikes
Each blade of grass anew: a new scent
Renewed sense
A new feeling to experience
Since others pass
Sense others' pasts
Then becomes a new since
Eagerly absorbing each scent
Content with relegating now to the past

Because she knows
It's always time to go.
On to the next...

Each step, with tail stiffened or breezy
Marking her territory briefly, neatly
Others trail easily
Wagging tales of precaution in her direction
She ignores at her discretion
Some say she's untrained, untamed
Though with shrewd precision
She always makes her destination

An adventurous soul
Sometimes careless and blithely unaware
Trusting herself to escape dangers
Though, no true threat has yet to appear

A careful trot around corners
A slip up and down hillsides
A stretch in open, empty fields
A full sprint to new sights

A pause to make a greeting
Mouth agape
Her tired tongue, teeth scrapes
A smile as if to say
"If you can't even keep up
What makes you think you can lead me?"

Then she runs with pride
Galloping eagerly
Stretching her stride

Wild, curious, free

All the ways to describe
A dog without a leash
Or a woman without a ring...

Dinner with Lorelei (3/31)

Let's recap
Pretend promises can't be broken
That friendships and thereof, tokens
Are infinite and redemptive
And conversations that range from
Religion to love
Are reflections, nay conceptions
Of devotion either way

Like talks of goals and drive
And ways we've had to survive
And plans we make to thrive
And days we feel most alive

"Does perfection exist? Give me an example of it"
And I'd foolhardily reminisce on a moment
Outside of this
To me, perfection is a memory
And John had taught me
By the time I'd recognize it, it'd be gone
It's as circular as a pop song
While conversing
I'd sing to bring unrehearsed verses
To the surface
"You remind me of what I really am"

There it is. Like untrained hand gestures
And subtle reminders of services closing
For two verbose souls
Who hadn't noticed the forward motions...
We'd discovered something new together:

Perfection, like peace, exists
Just beyond the reach of expectations.

74 (4/8)

If it's already broken
Why not break it more beautifully

Don't do that
Dangle Hope before my eyes
Tell me there's a way to my dreams
Moments before
I'd decided to abandon them completely
Don't keep me beholden to some future
Some vision
Then force me to bring it to fruition
To test my own limits
And expand my own ambitions
I'd just committed to being nihilistic
Erode this fork in my road
Make my journey easy, free me
Let me just be

64 (4/18)

Breathe. Release. Today feels like a new me
The sunset, a new beast
An era where night terrors flee
And morning brings renewed peace

I've been working on myself

If my thoughts are an echo chamber
Let my accolades resonate
Let the best of me take shape
Releasing myself from expectations

I've been listening a lot

Remembering old thoughts
About hopeful futures
That was once lost
Learning, true. But being critical of what's taught
When I truly take stock
And see I own everything once sought
How could I possibly doubt
That I'd ever get all that I want

59 (4/23)

The rearrangement is taking place
My future is taking shape
I'm walking in her

The math ain't mathing
The hour glass can't capture
The urgency within me to deliver
I'm there with you counting
Changing, mounting

Here's the hard part
The evaluation of all that's taking place
After the high of blithe optimism
The results take shape
Were they as expected? What next must be changed?
What patterns can we make sense of?
What still does not add up?

There is no quiet here
Insects tear through the tranquility
Teasing me
A silent Saturday was never truly in my reach
I didn't want to hear it anyways

So I'm up at 3 am
Watching the waves rush and the trees bend
Feeling the smoke flow outside and within
How dare my thoughts drift to you!
Are you just a ghost? Another goal?

A serotonin shot in the dark
How dare I see your face, trace your scars
Assume the truths within your heart
Imagine the strength and warmth of your arms
Remember the grace in your charm
When, by all measures that matter
We are so very far apart

First be worse (4/29)

Sometimes you have to sit and listen
To all the things you've gotten wrong
And you can choose to ignore it
It's no one's favorite song
But if you expect to do better
You've got to first be worse
In those regards, though at odds
Growth is a blessing and a curse

37 (5/15)

The signs are all there
Pointing the way
And enough kind words
Are floating towards me
I'd once lamented not having my applause
And now it's so loud, I fear I'm not a worthy cause

Doubt is healthy insofar that it keeps feet planted
But I will not use my fear as an excuse to stop expanding
I know there'll be flaws, and forthcoming damage
But for every sized scar, there is a bandage

I will manage. I can handle it.

35 (5/17)

Hard earned lessons learned
May be the only ones worth passing on
I'm glad to be of value

Finally seeing I'm proud to
Take the pains of yesterday
And help make sense of tomorrow

I'd once called myself a student
And in a lot of ways, that may still be true
But I'm glad to get to teach some

We live day to day, swayed by waves
That's the flow of ideas and emotions
I don't think we're meant to keep them

To ourselves. What good is the well
If you're the only one who's drinking?
Don't leave your friends in the drought
If your grass is green
Take your spout and start sprinkling

33 (5/19)

I awoke with an answer
As clear as the sky above
It must've come from above
There's no way I would've wanted that conclusion
It was right, however
However clever I see myself to be
No matter the work I'm willing to do
There's no point
In chasing my own tail
I've heard wonderful tales
I'd sold to myself
Hands remain empty
It's tempting, picturing
It's even sweeter remembering
There's something greater meant for me

The righteous believer (5/20)

The final leg, the home stretch
The new beginning, the last ditch
I'm both tired and excited
Cast aside those who've served their purpose
Not saying I'm perfect
Maybe even the opposite
But too many flaws in the same place
Regressing at the same pace
How easily one would be swayed
And I'd rather focus on the new day

Self-proclaimed genius is self destruction
What is change without disruption?
Excessive self image conflated as gumption

What is a visionary to those seeking stability?
A nuisance
I'd broken through the nooses
Only to rest and relish in the newness
My hands have not even begun
So far from being unsung
What happens to the Icarus who follows the Son?
Do they burn all the same?
Are they emboldened by the flame?
Justify the pain as redemption
Never mention doubts within their convictions
Rationalize contradiction
They, maybe alone, get it

Pending (5/24)

I see the remnants of a full life
Shelter from rain
A lawn to enjoy the blue skies
Receipts from adventures near and far
Maintenance costs
A trail to walk on
A path to call my own
A Lord to love me
And goals dangling above me
Though, nothing seems out of reach
What if I'm already fulfilled?
What fuels the content?
It's always nice to skim
With just enough sense
To whisper these things
Wise enough to keep my wins and losses to myself
Basking in joy, outwardly coy
Because I know someone's listening
One way or another
And this isn't for anyone other

I know I think too much
And today
I'm tired of trying to make sense of the world
Allow me to sit in the uncertainty
Feel
And prepare for tomorrow
Unresolved.

9 (6/12)

...and here I sit
With my wish list and yet accomplished promises
Chalking out new routines for my wellbeing
It's dazing how things end and begin
And end again
Dreams lead to goals
And relentlessly checking boxes
I know this life is a blessing
And I've got to keep marching
Finally found my own beat
And appreciate my clocking

No more eyeing the hourglass
My past isn't a haunting.
My future isn't daunting.
No other version of myself taunting.
No need for boasting or flaunting.
I am who I am. It is what it is.
And man, it is amazing.
Lord, allow me to be gracious and grateful.
Constantly in awe of your greatness.
I honestly and earnestly can't even imagine
What's awaiting.

12 (7/3)

I'm no longer interested in
Lamenting things that I don't have
When I have so much
When I am complete and whole
And safe and thriving
Alone.

Goes the spoils (7/26)

I'd like to write you
Out of existence
Pull you out of every crevice
In which you imprinted
Pull back my knees
From their displacements

I still can't quite believe
All the ways you've changed me

My reactions held me captive
And my explanations cemented your placement
What's all this wonder you've created?
And now, merely days in,
What is this melancholy I'm encased in?

What am I offering? Thought partnership?
Already fumbling through the intensity
Why would you ever pick me?
The prickly, whose softness was offered
And insisted withdrawn
A heart begging to be broken
Arms and legs hedging to be opened
A hopeless token

I'd imagined us making love
Questioning if I were enough
And seeking reassurance in your touch
I'd prefix our sex with
"I know you've been with
Women more beautiful than me"
These were MY words
Spoken in MY fantasy

How'd I become second fiddle in my own daydream?
How'd I manifest insecurities in my own sheets?
In the moments before my eyes closed to the world
Before I shut my brain to the outside.

How'd you become the one?
The aim, the goal, the vision?
Because we aligned on a mission.
Because you read my mind without permission.
Spoke the words I'd never heard.

Upon reverb, and after striking a nerve
Then took my time to listen with insistence
Bare minimum shit when I list it
And what did I give then?
A storm, a warning, a forlorn apology and grief, silence
And then I gifted distance.

So this is it
The truth behind the image and resistance
You are imperfect, I know it.
I can etch out your every weakness
Starting with your persistent indifference
I, like a mime, keep hitting the walls of your heart
The boundaries of your guard
But I know this all
And it excites me either way

How do you not see our greatness?
How could you ignore
These aches
And awakenings
And coincidences
And revelations
All associated with my name?

I want to be with you
And I want you to want the same.
Who wouldn't, after all?
Look at all I am...
Look at all I have to offer...

A note to self in late September (9/26)

This seems to be an inflection point
Where you relearn self-reliance
But your independence isn't tethered in pain
Your isolation isn't in defiance
Sometimes we must hibernate
Run fervently towards the quiet
Observe the whirlwind world grow chaotic
Tend to and mend wounds. In silence.

Sense (10/12)

I'm rethinking love these days
As if there is no limit
To the mosaic
Within the fabric of my being
What if there's space for it all?
For the adoration and the hatred
The give and take
The boastful pontification
And quiet contemplation
What if staying is the key to escaping...
The confines of my very own mind
How does liberation taste then?

Give me your hand.

My philosophy is not much bigger
Than happy feelings
And counting all the stars
My power comes from
The rhymes I've turned to poetry
Transcribing an Untitled rival
To the greatest manuscripts of survival
Letting my hope guide to
Joy unbridled, and undenied truths
And on this journey, learning
The world is misshapen clay
Soft and awaiting mindful creation

Grasp around my fingers
And feel my pulse quicken

Give me your ear.

Your choice to voice
Stay silent or make noise

I'm here to hear
And draw nearer to the source
Of course, the chorus
Echoes through my soul
And I hear it
your spirit, the lyrics
No wonder we get along
You are my favorite song

Feel it, my lips drawing nearer
And wide into a pensive smile

Give me it all.

The Friday night trouble man
The calming Saturday morning
We can be a weekend
And weaken the strong arm
Of the Sunday evening alarms
I crave the mundane
A mid-day stroll on a Monday
A tea-time toast on a Tuesday
A restful Thursday
After honoring Wednesday's namesake
I want it all—a senseless adventure

And maybe. Just maybe.
I can have it
If I just made space for love to inhabit
Not succumb to the same bad habits
And receive this existence as a gift
With all its serenity and madnesses
It's built here already
Within my very fabric

Grab it.

Single tear on smiley face emoji (11/7)

It's a really weird feeling
Being ghosted by my therapist
But I'm oddly smiling
Because it fits my trauma narrative

Where will you be
When my fear of abandonment
Rears its ugly head again?

Probably not there... that's the joke babe

It's okay
It doesn't stoke rage
It's hard to lament a new chapter
When you're crafting your own page

So cheers to all the lone rangers
The quiet cowgirls
The anxious day traders
The introverted poets
Crafting heartfelt verses
Bringing tears to complete strangers
While simultaneously cataloging
Their own fears and dangers

A passing thought (11/20)

Fear me
As you should
A woman who's worth it
Who's imperfect
But pursues her purpose in earnest
A woman with soft curves and sharp words
Whose lips speak sweet curses
And rehearses Bible verses
With equal force and urgency

Left hand gently crafts in cursive
Right hand punches the earth
Feet firmly planted at uncrossed lines
Head drifting with the clouds in the sky
A smile that shines and eyes that cry
Dependent upon the wind, and the why

So fear it all
The peace and the war
The heat and the cold
Just don't be afraid of being
A human being
And admitting the things
You're unprepared to speak
Or even scared to think

I don't know who needs to hear this (11/26)

I don't. For real.
I haven't done the analysis
To capture my audience's madness
To create that perfectly-timed message
That seems the universe crafted the magic

What do you need to hear dear?
That everything will be alright?
That time will surpass this fright?
That you're never really alone
While you toss and turn in an empty bed at night?

That no matter how deeply the darkness stirs inside
We're all still bending toward the light?

The world is surprisingly safe and warm
Depending on how you set your sights

Right?

I don't know who needs to hear this
So I'll start with myself
Who knows the deep-rooted turmoil
Of anyone else?

We're all the same, in that way.

To those ears that await
I hope this message makes it
And resonates

It will be okay.

Sunday (12/4)

You will unearth every deep-seeded fear
As you till through the weeds
Within your own heart
You're here for a reason
Not simply treason
Against your own accord
Tell yourself yourself is yours

...days later (12/15)

I found your shirt in my laundry
Somehow you found a way to haunt me
It fits me snug, like a fully-formed hug
At least I recall your touch fondly
I won't lie and claim ease
As if my life moved on with the breeze
Like I didn't have to cry
And remind myself to breathe
Getting extra sleep
Playing sad songs to sing along
Forgetting to eat
It took a few days to fight through the haze
But I think I've stumbled upon a truth
I feel more like myself today
Now
That I've lost you

(And I don't want to reopen doors
Or even trigger more hurt
So you may never know
That I'm sitting here now
Wearing your shirt)

Unresolved (12/19)

I've done these things alone before
And felt a curious joy
The sounds aren't new
Neither the smell nor feel

Am I seeking him from a place of scarcity?
Willing to overlook flaws glaringly
For fear no one else will care for me?
Name it.

Am I trying to fit a narrative?
Of success that's been elusive?
"You can't have it all"
Seemed more like a challenge
Than a harsh truth passed down by elders
Claim it.

I do the math, it is my job
To see all the ways
My personhood has been robbed
Is it revenge or a rewrite
To assuage fears of the youth
Who see themselves in my plight?
Is that right?
Frame it.

Tonight is cold
My skin already thickening
And yet through the haze
I found time to make conversation
With a stranger
As I once did before

Overdue escape (12/28)

I'm no wiser than the mountain
    That let's the snow fall down its peak
        To the frozen ground beneath
I'm no smarter than the trees
    Who cast aside their leaves
        And let go of branches that no longer serve them
How'd I learn to ignore the sun?
    That makes distance and changes days
        And returns when it is ready

Estes Park (12/31)

And as I've grown
I've toured
The same lands that my father explored
Places he'd taken me before
Seemed a lot less scary
Perhaps that's growth

And in my youth
I'd grasp his hand when I was afraid
Covered my eyes to things too big
Now I watch mountains shrink at my wake
Perhaps that's what it means to get older

Closure (Today)

She thinks she knows she's had enough
Of lowering her guard then acting tough
Of saying too little too much
Covering her mouth when making love

She wrapped her legs around his
And with her full weight, took him in
As if redemption existed
In the space between them
So she'd open and close
Whatever she could control

Yet in their throes
In their silence about their roles
The lack of lust or luster
Lost her
Neither his touch
Nor thrust could rush her
She knew then
What she'd only seen
In passing thoughts before
She's no longer being allured by the lore
The truth was as clear as her fading torch
She had asked for more and he'd ignored
Then she grew bored...

He said
"Let's just enjoy the moment we had"
And in her exhaustion, she relented
She'd meant to say "I love you"
But knew it was "goodbye" in disguise
And that bothered her
How easily she could relate
And conflate the two

So instead she sighed
And crept out in silence

She knows she'll think about the leaving
Cleaving a new dream and releasing
Things he would never provide
Yet somehow it didn't matter
The prospect of being alone again
Neither frightened nor saddened her
That indifference cemented the decision

Women with direction
Often face
Rigid crossroads

Women with ambition
Are served by fate
Nights alone

Women with drive
Can't escape
Empty homes

And who is she?
But a woman
With hefty sights
A woman
With heavy light

Acknowledgements

Thanks to Andrea Wofford for her amazing cover design skills.

Thanks to Sarah Beach for her meticulous copyediting.

Thanks also to Sean Petrie and Burlwood Books for bringing this work, my words, my voice to life and new heights. Special shout out to the entire Typewriter Rodeo family for their support and love of the beautiful art of poetry.

About the Author

LaCole Foots loves to learn about the world and uses her poetry to sift through some of the biggest questions we all face and dreams we all share. Her self-published poetry anthology, *Durance*, is a collection of coping with grief, healing, and finding oneself in the process.

She is continuing to explore these big themes and more in her current projects and sees HEAVY LIGHT as a milestone in her journey.

She has an analytical background with an MPA from Carnegie Mellon University, and when not writing poetry, she is storytelling through data as a data strategist at her analytics firm. More at www.LaColeFoots.com

Burlwood Books is a small independent press in Austin, Texas. We are dedicated to art that celebrates the messy, vibrant, mistake-filled wonder of life.

www.ingramcontent.com/pod-product-compliance
Lightning Source LLC
Chambersburg PA
CBHW030511130626
46549CB00007B/2947